# SAFE *in th*
## SHEPHERD'S ARMS

*Hope and Encouragement from Psalm 23*

# MAX LUCADO

GIFT BOOKS
*from Hallmark*

BOK5067

COUNTRYMAN

Published under license from J. Countryman®, a division of Thomas Nelson, Inc,
Nashville, Tennessee 37214, exclusively for Hallmark Cards, Inc.

Compiled and edited by Terri Gibbs

Editorial Supervision: Karen Hill, Administrative Editor for Max Lucado

Designed by UDG|DesignWorks, Sisters, Oregon.

ISBN: 1-4041-00253

www.hallmark.com
www.jcountryman.com

Printed and bound in the China

FOR PAT HILE

Celebrating twenty years of faithful
service to the same flock.

# Contents

Come to me," God invites, "all of you who are weary and carry heavy burdens, and I will give you rest" (Matt. 11:28 NLT).

If we let him, God will lighten our loads . . . but how do we let him? May I invite an old friend to show us? The Twenty-third Psalm.

*The LORD is my shepherd;*
*I shall not want.*
*He makes me to lie down in green pastures;*
*He leads me beside the still waters.*
*He restores my soul;*
*He leads me in the paths of righteousness*
*For His name's sake.*
*Yea, though I walk through the valley of the*
*shadow of death, I will fear no evil;*
*For You are with me;*
*Your rod and Your staff, they comfort me.*

*You prepare a table before me in the presence of my enemies;*
*You anoint my head with oil;*
*My cup runs over.*
*Surely goodness and mercy shall follow me*
*All the days of my life;*
*And I will dwell in the house of the Lord Forever.* (NKJV)

Do more beloved words exist? Framed and hung in hospital halls, scratched on prison walls, quoted by the young, and whispered by the dying. In these lines sailors have found a harbor, the frightened have found a father, and strugglers have found a friend.

And because the passage is so deeply loved, it is widely known. Can you find ears on which these words have never fallen? Set to music in a hundred songs, translated into a thousand tongues, domiciled in a million hearts.

One of those hearts might be yours.

— MAX LUCADO

# THE LORD IS MY SHEPHERD

The psalmist rejoiced to say,
"The Lord is my shepherd,"
and in so doing he proudly implied,
"I am his sheep."

Why did David write the Twenty-third Psalm? To build our trust in God . . . to remind us of who he is. God is Yahweh—an unchanging God, an uncaused God, and an ungoverned God.

When Lloyd Douglas, author of *The Robe* and other novels, attended college, he lived in a boardinghouse. A retired, wheelchair-bound music professor resided on the first floor. Each morning Douglas would stick his head in the door of the teacher's apartment and ask the same question, "Well, what's the good news?" The old man would pick up his tuning fork, tap it on the side of the wheelchair, and say, "That's middle C! It was middle C yesterday; it will be middle C tomorrow; it will be middle C a thousand years from now. The tenor upstairs sings flat. The piano across the hall is out of tune, but, my friend, that is middle C." [1]

You and I need a middle C. Haven't you had enough change in your life? Relationships change. Health changes. The weather changes. But the Yahweh who ruled the earth last night is the same Yahweh who rules it today. Same convictions. Same plan. Same mood. Same love. He never changes. You can no more alter God than a pebble can alter the rhythm of the Pacific. Yahweh is our middle C. A still point in a turning world. Don't we need a still point? Don't we need an unchanging shepherd?

We equally need an uncaused shepherd. No one breathed life into Yahweh. No one sired him. No one gave birth to him. No one caused him. No act brought him forth.

Though he creates, God was never created. Though he makes, he was never made. Though he causes, he was never caused. Hence the psalmist's proclamation: "Before the mountains were born or you brought forth the earth and the world, from everlasting to everlasting you are God" (Ps. 90:2 NIV). . . .

God—our Shepherd—doesn't check the weather; he makes it. He doesn't defy gravity; he created it. He isn't affected by health; he has no body. Jesus said, "God is spirit" (John 4:24). Since he has no body, he has no limitations—equally active in Cambodia as he is in Connecticut. "Where can I go to get away from your Spirit?" asked David. "Where can I run from you? If I go up to the heavens, you are there. If I lie down in the grave, you are there" (Ps. 139:7–8).

Since no act brought him forth, no act can take him out. Does he fear an earthquake? Does he tremble at a tornado? Hardly. Yahweh sleeps through storms and calms the winds with a word.

Cancer does not trouble him and cemeteries do not disturb him. He was here before they came. He'll be here after they are gone. . . .

Counselors can comfort you in the storm, but you need a God who can still the storm. Friends can hold your hand at your deathbed, but you need a Yahweh who has defeated the grave. Philosophers can debate the meaning of life, but you need a Lord who can declare the meaning of life.

You need a Yahweh.

You don't need what Dorothy found. Remember her discovery in The Wonderful Wizard of Oz? She and her trio followed the yellow-brick road only to discover that the wizard was a wimp! Nothing but smoke and mirrors and tin-drum thunder. Is that the kind of god you need?

You don't need to carry the burden of a lesser god . . . a god on a shelf, a god in a box, or a god in a bottle. No, you need a God who can place 100 billion stars in our galaxy and 100 billion galaxies in the universe. You need a God who can shape two fists of flesh into 75 to 100 billion nerve cells, each with as many as 10,000 connections to other nerve cells, place it in a skull, and call it a brain.

And you need a God who, while so mind-numbingly mighty, can come in the soft of night and touch you with the tenderness of an April snow.

You need a Yahweh.

And, according to David, you have one. He is your shepherd.

TRAVELING LIGHT

You are a great God.

Your character is holy.

Your truth is absolute.

Your strength is unending.

Your discipline is fair. . . .

Your provisions are abundant for our needs.

Your light is adequate for our path.

Your grace is sufficient for our sins. . . .

You are never early, never late. . . .

You sent your Son in the fullness of time and

will return at the consummation of time.

Your plan is perfect.

Bewildering. Puzzling. Troubling.

But perfect.


from "He Reminded Us of You"
(a prayer for a friend)

# I Shall Not Want

*What you have
in your Shepherd is greater than
what you don't have in life.*

David has found the pasture where discontent goes to die. It's as if he is saying, "What I have in God is greater than what I don't have in life."

You think you and I could learn to say the same?

Think for just a moment about the things you own. Think about the house you have, the car you drive, the money you've saved. Think about the jewelry you've inherited and the stocks you've traded and the clothes you've purchased. Envision all your stuff, and let me remind you of two biblical truths.

Your stuff isn't yours. Ask any coroner. Ask any embalmer. Ask any funeral-home director. No one takes anything with him. When one of the wealthiest men in history, John D. Rockefeller, died, his accountant was asked, "How much did

John D. leave?" The accountant's reply? "All of it."

"Naked a man comes from his mother's womb, and as he comes, so he departs. He takes nothing from his labor that he can carry in his hand" (Eccles. 5:15 NIV).

All that stuff—it's not yours. And you know what else about all that stuff? It's not you. Who you are has nothing to do with the clothes you wear or the car you drive. Jesus said, "Life is not defined by what you have, even when you have a lot" (Luke 12:15 MSG). Heaven does not know you as the fellow with the nice suit or the woman with the big house or the kid with the new bike. Heaven knows your heart. "The Lord does not look at the things man looks at. Man looks at the outward appearance, but the Lord looks at the heart" (1 Sam. 16:7 NIV). When God thinks of you, he may see your compassion, your devotion, your tenderness or quick mind, but he doesn't think of your things. . . .

You have a God who hears you, the power of love behind you, the Holy Spirit within you, and all of heaven ahead of you. If you have the Shepherd, you have grace for every sin, direction for every turn, a candle for every corner, and an anchor for every storm. You have everything you need.

You and I could pray like the Puritan. He sat down to a meal of bread and water. He bowed his head and declared, "All this and Jesus too?"

Can't we be equally content? Paul says that "godliness with contentment is great gain" (1 Tim. 6:6 NIV). When we surrender to God the cumbersome sack of discontent, we don't just give up something; we gain something. God replaces it with a lightweight, tailor-made, sorrow-resistant attaché of gratitude.

What will you gain with contentment? You

may gain your marriage. You may gain precious hours with your children. You may gain your self-respect. You may gain joy. You may gain the faith to say, "The Lord is my shepherd; I shall not want."

TRAVELING LIGHT

# HE MAKES
# ME TO LIE DOWN IN
# GREEN PASTURES

*Nestle deeply*
*in the tall shoots of his love,*
*and there you will*
*find rest.*

For sheep to sleep, everything must be just right. No predators. No tension in the flock. No bugs in the air. No hunger in the belly. Everything has to be just so.

Unfortunately, sheep cannot find safe pasture, nor can they spray insecticide, deal with the frictions, or find food. They need help. They need a shepherd to "lead them" and help them "lie down in green pastures." Without a shepherd, they can't rest.

Without a shepherd, neither can we.

In the second verse of the Twenty-third Psalm, David the poet becomes David the artist. His quill becomes a brush, his parchment a canvas, and his words paint a picture. A flock of sheep on folded legs, encircling a shepherd. Bellies nestled deep in the long shoots of grass. A still pond on one side, the watching shepherd on the other. "He makes me to lie down in green pastures; He leads me beside the still waters" (Ps. 23:2 NKJV).

Note the two pronouns preceding the two verbs. *He* makes me . . . *He* leads me . . .

Who is the active one? Who is in charge? The shepherd. The shepherd selects the trail and prepares the pasture. The sheep's job—our job—is to watch the shepherd. With our eyes on our Shepherd, we'll be able to get some sleep. "You will keep him in perfect peace, whose mind is stayed on You" (Isa. 26:3 NKJV). . . .

For you to be healthy, you must rest. Slow down, and God will heal you. He will bring rest to your mind, to your body, and most of all to your soul. He will lead you to green pastures.

Green pastures were not the natural terrain of Judea. The hills around Bethlehem where David kept his flock were not lush and green. Even today they are white and parched. Any green pasture in Judea is the work of some shepherd. He has cleared the rough, rocky land. Stumps have been torn out, and brush has been burned. Irrigation. Cultivation. Such are the work of a shepherd.

Hence, when David says, "He makes me to lie down in green pastures," he is saying, "My shepherd makes me lie down in his finished work." With his own pierced hands, Jesus created a pasture for the soul. He tore out the thorny underbrush of condemnation. He pried loose the huge boulders of sin. In their place he planted seeds of grace and dug ponds of mercy.

And he invites us to rest there. Can you imagine the satisfaction in the heart of the shepherd when, with work completed, he sees his sheep rest in the tender grass?

Can you imagine the satisfaction in the heart of God when we do the same? His pasture is his gift to us. This is not a pasture that you have made. Nor is it a pasture that you deserve. It is a gift of God.

TRAVELING LIGHT

To recognize God as Lord is to acknowledge that he is sovereign and supreme in the universe. To accept him as Savior is to accept his gift of salvation offered on the cross. To regard him as Father is to go a step further. Ideally, a father is the one in your life who provides and protects. That is exactly what God has done.

God has proven himself as a faithful father. Now it falls to us to be trusting children.

HE STILL MOVES STONES

# HE LEADS ME BESIDE THE STILL WATERS

*God leads us.*
*God will do the right thing*
*at the right time.*

He leads me beside the still waters," David declares. And, in case we missed the point, he repeats the phrase in the next verse: "He leads me in the paths of righteousness."

"He leads me." God isn't behind me, yelling, "Go!" He is ahead of me, bidding, "Come!" He is in front, clearing the path, cutting the brush, showing the way. Just before the curve, he says, "Turn here." Prior to the rise, he motions, "Step up here." Standing next to the rocks, he warns, "Watch your step here."

He leads us. He tells us what we need to know when we need to know it. As a New Testament writer would affirm: "We will find grace to help us *when we need it*" (Heb. 4:16 NLT, emphasis mine).

God leads us. God will do the right thing at the right time. And what a difference that makes. . . .

God is leading you. Leave tomorrow's problems until tomorrow.

Arthur Hays Sulzberger was the publisher of the New York Times during the Second World War. Because of the world conflict, he found it almost impossible to sleep. He was never able to banish worries from his mind until he adopted as his motto these five words—"one step enough for me"—taken from the hymn "Lead Kindly Light."[2]

*Lead, kindly Light . . .*
*Keep Thou my feet; I do not ask to see*
*the distant scene; one step enough for me.*

God isn't going to let you see the distant scene either. So you might as well quit looking for it. He promises a lamp unto our feet, not a crystal ball into the future (Ps. 119:105). We do not need to know what will happen tomorrow. We only need to know he leads us and "we will find grace to help us when we need it" (Heb. 4:16 NLT).

TRAVELING LIGHT

We need to hear that God is still in control. We need to hear that it's not over until he says so. We need to hear that life's mishaps and tragedies are not a reason to bail out. They are simply a reason to sit tight.

Corrie ten Boom used to say, "When the train goes through a tunnel and the world gets dark, do you jump out? Of course not. You sit still and trust the engineer to get you through."

Next time you're disappointed, don't panic.

Don't jump out. Don't give up. Just be patient and let God remind you he's still in control. It ain't over till it's over.

He Still Moves Stones

# HE RESTORES
# MY SOUL

*Jesus restores our*
*hope by giving us himself.*

It's hard to see things grow old. The town in which I grew up is growing old. . . . Some of the buildings are boarded up. Some of the houses are torn down. . . . The old movie house where I took my dates has "For Sale" on the marquee. . . .

I wish I could make it all new again. I wish I could blow the dust off the streets . . . but I can't.

I can't. But God can. "He restores my soul," wrote the shepherd. He doesn't reform; he restores. He doesn't camouflage the old; he restores the new. The Master Builder will pull out the original plan and restore it. He will restore the vigor. He will restore the energy. He will restore the hope. He will restore the soul.

THE APPLAUSE OF HEAVEN

For many people, life is—well, life is a jungle. Not a jungle of trees and beasts. Would that it were so simple. Would that our jungles could be cut with a machete or our adversaries trapped in a cage. But our jungles are comprised of the thicker thickets of failing health, broken hearts, and empty wallets. Our forests are framed with hospital walls and divorce courts. We don't hear the screeching of birds or the roaring of lions, but we do hear the complaints of neighbors and the demands of bosses. Our predators are our creditors, and the brush that surrounds us is the rush that exhausts us.

It's a jungle out there.

And for some, even for many, hope is in short supply. . . .

What would it take to restore your hope? . . .

Our Shepherd majors in restoring hope to the soul. Whether you are a lamb lost on a craggy ledge or a city slicker alone in a deep jungle, everything changes when your rescuer appears.

Your loneliness diminishes, because you have fellowship.

Your despair decreases, because you have vision.

Your confusion begins to lift, because you have direction.

Please note: You haven't left the jungle. The trees still eclipse the sky, and the thorns still cut the skin. Animals lurk and rodents scurry. The jungle is still a jungle. It hasn't changed, but you have. You have changed because you have hope. And you have hope because you have met someone who can lead you out.

Your Shepherd knows that you were not made for this place. He knows you are not equipped for this place. So he has come to guide you out.

He has come to restore your soul. . . .

Jesus doesn't give hope by changing the jungle; he restores our hope by giving us himself. And he has promised to stay until the very end. "I am with you always, to the very end of the age" (Matt. 28:20 NIV).

TRAVELING LIGHT

# HE LEADS ME IN PATHS OF RIGHTEOUSNESS

*The path of righteousness*
*is a narrow, winding trail up a steep hill.*
*At the top of the hill is a cross.*

Jesus called himself the Good Shepherd. The Shepherd who knows his sheep by name and lays down his life for them. The Shepherd who protects, provides, and possesses his sheep. The Bible is replete with this picture of God.

> "The Lord is my shepherd" (Ps. 23:1).

> "We are your people, the sheep of your flock" (Ps. 79:13).

> "He made us, and we belong to him; we are his people, the sheep he tends" (Ps. 100:3).

The imagery is carried over to the New Testament.

He is the shepherd who will risk his life to save the one straying sheep (see Luke 15:4).

He has pity on people because they are like sheep without a shepherd (see Matt. 9:36).

His disciples are his flock (see Luke 12:32.)

When the shepherd is attacked, the sheep are scattered (see Matt. 26:31).

He is the shepherd of the souls of men (see 1 Peter 2:25).

He is the great shepherd of the sheep (see Heb. 13:20).

Eighty percent of Jesus' listeners made their living off of the land. Many were shepherds. They lived on the mesa with the sheep. No flock ever grazed without a shepherd, and no shepherd was ever off duty. When sheep wandered, the shepherd found them. When they fell, he carried them. When they were hurt, he healed them.

Sheep aren't smart. They tend to wander into running creeks for water, then their wool grows heavy and they drown. They need a shepherd to lead them to "calm water" (Ps. 23:2). They have no natural defense—no claws, no horns, no fangs. They are helpless. Sheep need a shepherd with a "rod and . . . walking stick" (Ps. 23:4) to protect them. They have no sense of direction. They need someone to lead them "on paths that are right" (Ps. 23:3).

So do we. We, too, tend to be swept away by waters we should have avoided. We have no defense against the evil lion who prowls about seeking who he might devour. We, too, get lost. "We all have wandered away like sheep; each of us has gone his own way" (Isa. 53:6).

We need a shepherd. We don't need a cowboy

to herd us; we need a shepherd to care for us and to guide us.

   And we have one. One who knows us by name.

A GENTLE THUNDER

# FOR HIS
# NAME'S SAKE

*If you want
to touch God's heart,
use the name he loves to hear.
Call him Father.*

God is the one who heals. He may use a branch of medicine and a branch of a hospital or a branch of a live oak tree, but he is the one who takes the poison out of the system. He is *Jehovah-rophe*.

He is also *Jehovah-nissi,* the Lord my banner. . . .

These are just a few of the names of God that describe his character. Study them, for in any given day, you may need each one of them. Let me show you what I mean.

When you're confused about the future, go to your *Jehovah-raah*, your caring shepherd. When you're anxious about provision, talk to *Jehovah-jireh,* the Lord who provides. Are your challenges too great? Seek the help of *Jehovah-shalom,* the Lord is peace. Is your body sick? Are your emotions weak?

*Jehovah-rophe,* the Lord who heals you, will see you now. Do you feel like a soldier stranded behind enemy lines? Take refuge in *Jehovah-nissi,* the Lord my banner.

Meditating on the names of God reminds you of the character of God. Take these names and bury them in your heart.

God is

the shepherd who guides,

the Lord who provides,

the voice who brings peace in the storm,

the physician who heals the sick, and

the banner that guides the soldier.

THE GREAT HOUSE OF GOD

# YEA, THOUGH I WALK THROUGH THE VALLEY OF THE SHADOW OF DEATH

*He gathers the lambs
in his arms and carries them
close to his heart.*

———

ISAIAH 40:11 NIV

Summer in ancient Palestine. A woolly bunch of bobbing heads follow the shepherd out of the gate. The morning sun has scarcely crested the horizon, and he is already leading his flock. Like every other day, he guides them through the gate and out into the fields. But unlike most days, the shepherd will not return home tonight. He will not rest on his bed, and the sheep will not sleep in their fenced-in pasture. This is the day the shepherd takes the sheep to the high country. Today he leads his flock to the mountains.

He has no other choice. Springtime grazing has left his pasture bare, so he must seek new fields. With no companion other than his sheep and no desire other than their welfare, he leads them to the deep grass of the hillsides. The shepherd and his flock will be gone for weeks, perhaps months. They will stay well into the autumn, until the grass is gone and the chill is unbearable.

Not all shepherds make this journey. The trek is long. The path is dangerous. Poisonous plants can infect the flock. Wild animals can attack the flock. There are narrow trails and dark valleys. Some shepherds choose the security of the barren pasture below.

But the good shepherd doesn't. He knows the path. He has walked this trail many times. Besides, he is prepared. Staff in hand and rod attached to his belt. With his staff he will nudge the flock; with his rod he will protect and lead the flock. He will lead them to the mountains.

David understood this annual pilgrimage. Before he led Israel, he led sheep. And could his time as a shepherd be the inspiration behind one of the greatest verses in the Bible? "Yea, though I walk through the valley of the shadow of death, I will fear no evil; for You are with me; Your rod and Your staff, they comfort me" (Ps. 23:4 NKJV).

For what the shepherd does with the flock, our Shepherd will do with us. He will lead us to the high country. When the pasture is bare down here, God will lead us up there. He will guide us through the gate, out of the flatlands, and up the path of the mountain.

Someday our Shepherd will take us to the mountain by way of the valley. He will guide us to his house through the valley of the shadow of death.

TRAVELING LIGHT

Growing older. Aging. We laugh about it, and we groan about it. We resist it, but we can't stop it. And with the chuckles and wrinkles come some serious thoughts and questions about what happens when we die. Is death when we go to sleep? Or is death when we finally wake up?

As a minister, I'm often asked to speak at funerals. I no longer have to ask the family what they want me to say; I already know. Oh, I may have to ask a question or two about the deceased, and that I do, but I don't ask them what they want me to say. I know.

They want to hear what God says about death. They want to hear how God would answer their questions about the life hereafter. They don't want my opinion; nor do they want the thoughts of a philosopher or the research of a scientist. They want to know what God says. If Jesus were here, at the head of this casket, in the middle of this cemetery, what would he say?

And so under the canopy of sorrow, I give God's words. I share the eulogy Jesus gave for himself.

The disciples did not know it was his farewell address. No one did, but it was. He knew he had just witnessed his final sunset. He knew death would come with the morning. So he spoke about death. Here is how be began.

> Don't let your hearts be troubled.
> Trust in God, and trust in me. There are many
> rooms in my Father's house; I would not tell you this if
> it were not true. I am going there to prepare a place
> for you. After I go and prepare a place for you,
> I will come back and take you to be with me
> so that you may be where I am.
>
> ———
>
> (1 JOHN 14:1–4).

What kind of statement is that? Trust me with your death. When you face the tomb, don't be troubled—trust me! You get the impression that to God the grave is a no-brainer. He speaks as casually as the mechanic who says to a worried client, "Sure, the engine needs an overhaul, but don't worry. I can do it." For us it's an ordeal. For him it's no big deal.

We must trust God. We must trust not only that he does what is best but that he knows what is ahead.

A GENTLE THUNDER

# I WILL
# FEAR NO EVIL

*When I am afraid,*
*I put my trust in you.*

———

PSALM 56:3 NLT

I will fear no evil." How could David make such a claim? Because he knew where to look. "You are with me; Your rod and Your staff, they comfort me."

Rather than turn to the other sheep, David turned to the Shepherd. Rather than stare at the problems, he stared at the rod and staff. Because he knew where to look, David was able to say, "I will fear no evil."

I know a fellow who has a fear of crowds. When encircled by large groups, his breath grows short, panic surfaces, and he begins to sweat like a sumo wrestler in a sauna. He received some help, curiously, from a golfing buddy.

The two were at a movie theatre, waiting their turn to enter, when fear struck again. The crowd closed in like a forest. He wanted out and out fast. His buddy told him to take a few deep breaths. Then he helped manage the crisis by reminding him of the golf course.

"When you are hitting your ball out of the rough, and you are surrounded by trees, what do you do?"

"I look for an opening."

"You don't stare at the trees?"

"Of course not. I find an opening and focus on hitting the ball through it."

"Do the same in the crowd. When you feel the panic, don't focus on the people; focus on the opening."

Good counsel in golf. Good counsel in life. Rather than focus on the fear, focus on the solution.

That's what Jesus did.

That's what David did.

And that's what the writer of Hebrews urges us

to do. "Let us run with endurance the race that is set before us, looking unto Jesus, the author and finisher of our faith" (Heb. 12:1–2 NKJV). . . .

Don't measure the size of the mountain; talk to the One who can move it. Instead of carrying the world on your shoulders, talk to the One who holds the universe on his. Hope is a look away.

Traveling Light

Faith is trusting
what the eye can't see.
Eyes see the prowling lion.
Faith sees Daniel's angel.
Eyes see storms. Faith sees Noah's rainbow.
Eyes see giants. Faith sees Canaan.
Your eyes see your faults.
Your faith sees your Savior.
Your eyes see your guilt.
Your faith sees his blood.
Your eyes see your grave.
Your faith sees a city whose
builder and maker is God.
Your eyes look in the mirror and
see a sinner, a failure, a promise-breaker.
But by faith you look in the mirror
and see a robed prodigal bearing the ring of
grace on your finger and the kiss of
your Father on your face.

When God Whispers Your Name

# THOU
# ART WITH ME

*I will not leave you.*

———

GENESIS 28:15

Y ou are with me."

Yes, you, Lord, are in heaven. Yes, you rule the universe. Yes, you sit upon the stars and make your home in the deep. But yes, yes, yes, you are with me.

The Lord is with me. The Creator is with me. Yahweh is with me.

Moses proclaimed it: "What great nation has a god as near to them as the Lord our God is near to us" (Deut. 4:7 NLT).

Paul announced it: "He is not far from each one of us" (Acts 17:27 NIV).

And . . . somewhere in the pasture, wilderness, or palace, David discovered that God meant business when he said:

"I will not leave you" (Gen. 28:15). . . .

The discovery of David is indeed the message of Scripture—the Lord is with us. And, since the Lord is near, everything is different. Everything!

You may be facing death, but you aren't facing death alone; the Lord is with you. You may be facing unemployment, but you aren't facing unemployment alone; the Lord is with you. You may be facing marital struggles, but you aren't facing them alone; the Lord is with you. You may be facing debt, but you aren't facing debt alone; the Lord is with you.

Underline these words: *You are not alone.*

Your family may turn against you, but God won't. Your friends may betray you, but God won't. You may feel alone in the wilderness, but you are not. He is with you.

TRAVELING LIGHT

# YOUR ROD
## AND YOUR STAFF,
## THEY COMFORT ME

*God has proven himself*
*a faithful father. Now it falls to us*
*to be trusting children.*

When I see a flock of sheep I see exactly that, a flock. A rabble of wool. A herd of hooves. I don't see a sheep. I see sheep. All alike. None different. That's what I see.

But not so with the shepherd. To him every sheep is different. Every face is special. Every face has a story. And every sheep has a name. The one with the sad eyes, that's Droopy. And the fellow with one ear up and the other down, I call him Oscar. And the small one with the black patch on his leg, he's an orphan with no brothers. I call him Joseph.

The shepherd knows his sheep. He calls them by name.

When we see a crowd, we see exactly that, a crowd. Filling a stadium or flooding a mall. When we see a crowd, we see people, not persons, but people. A herd of humans. A flock of faces. That's what we see.

But not so with the Shepherd. To him every face is different. Every face is a story. Every face is a child. Every child has a name. The one with the sad eyes, that's Sally. The old fellow with one eyebrow up and the other down, Harry's his name. And the young one with the limp? He's an orphan with no brothers. I call him Joey.

The Shepherd knows his sheep. He knows each one by name. The Shepherd knows you. He knows your name. And he will never forget it. "I have written your name on my hand" (Isa. 49:16).

Quite a thought, isn't it? Your name on God's hand. Your name on God's lips. Maybe you've seen your name in some special places. On an award or diploma or walnut door. Or maybe you've heard your name from some important people—a coach, a celebrity, a teacher. But to think that your name is on God's hand and on God's lips . . . my, could it be?

WHEN GOD WHISPERS YOUR NAME

Not only is your name written on God's hand but what matters to you matters to him. You probably think that's true when it comes to the big stuff. When it comes to the major-league difficulties like death, disease, sin, and disaster   you know that God cares.

But what about the smaller things? What about grouchy bosses or flat tires or lost dogs? What about broken dishes, late flights, toothaches, or a crashed hard disk? Do these matter to God?

I mean, he's got a universe to run. He's got the planets to keep balanced and presidents and kings to watch over. He's got wars to worry with and famines to fix. Who am I to tell him about my ingrown toenail?

I'm glad you asked. Let me tell you who you are. In fact, let me proclaim who you are.

> You are an heir of God and a co-heir with Christ (Rom. 8:17).
>
> You are eternal, like an angel (Luke 20:36).
>
> You have a crown that will last forever (1 Cor. 9:25).
>
> You are a holy priest (1 Pet. 2:5), a treasured possession (Exod. 19:5).
>
> You were chosen before the creation of the world (Eph. 1:4). You are destined for "praise, fame, and honor, and you will be a holy people to the Lord your God" (Deut. 26:19).

But more than any of the above—more significant than any title or position—is the simple fact that you are God's child. "The Father has loved us so much that we are called children of God. And we really are his children" (1 John 3:1).

I love that last phrase! "We really are his children." It's as if John knew some of us would shake our heads and say, "Naw, not me. Mother Teresa, maybe. Billy Graham, all right. But not me." If those are your feelings, John added that phrase for you.

"We really are his children."

As a result, if something is important to you, it's important to God.

He Still Moves Stones

# YOU PREPARE A TABLE BEFORE ME IN THE PRESENCE OF MY ENEMIES

*God is the shepherd*
*who guides, the Lord who provides,*
*the voice who brings peace*
*in the storm.*

At this point in the psalm, David's mind seems to be lingering in the high country with the sheep. Having guided the flock through the valley to the alp lands for greener grass, he remembers the shepherd's added responsibility. He must prepare the pasture.

This is new land, so the shepherd must be careful. Ideally, the grazing area will be flat, a mesa or tableland. The shepherd searches for poisonous plants and ample water. He looks for signs of wolves, coyotes, and bears.

Of special concern to the shepherd is the adder, a small brown snake that lives underground. Adders are known to pop out of their holes and nip the sheep on the nose. The bite often infects and can even kill. As defense against the snake, the shepherd pours a circle of oil at the top of each adder's hole. He also applies the oil to the noses of the animals. The oil on the snake's hole lubricates the exit, preventing the snake from climbing out. The smell of the oil on the sheep's nose drives the serpent away. The shepherd, in a very real sense, has prepared the table.[3]

What if your Shepherd did for you what the shepherd did for his flock? Suppose he dealt with your enemy, the devil, and prepared for you a safe place of nourishment? Suppose he, in the hour of your failure, invited you to a meal?

What would you say if I told you he has done exactly that?

TRAVELING LIGHT

You see, he has called us to himself and invited us to take a permanent place at his table. When we take our place next to the other sinners-made-saints . . . we share in God's glory.

May I share a partial list of what awaits you at his table?

You are beyond condemnation (Rom. 8:1).

You are delivered from the law (Rom. 7:6).

You are near God (Eph. 2:13).

You are delivered from the power of evil (Col. 1:13).

You are a member of his kingdom (Col. 1:13).

You are justified (Rom. 5:1).

You have access to God at any moment (Eph. 2:18).

You will never be abandoned (Heb. 13:5).

You possess (get this!) every spiritual blessing possible. "In Christ, God has given us every spiritual blessing in the heavenly world" (Eph. 1:3). This is the gift offered to the lowliest sinner on earth. Who could make such an offer but God?

IN THE GRIP OF GRACE

# YOU ANOINT
# MY HEAD WITH OIL

*When we come to God . . .*

*we come with high hopes and*

*a humble heart.*

In ancient Israel shepherds used oil for three
purposes: to repel insects, to prevent conflicts,
and to heal wounds.

Bugs bug people, but they can kill sheep. Flies,
mosquitoes, and gnats can turn the summer into a
time of torture for the livestock. Consider nose
flies, for example. If they succeed in depositing
their eggs into the soft membrane of the sheep's
nose, the eggs become worm-like larvae, which
drive the sheep insane. One shepherd explains:
"For relief from this agonizing annoyance sheep will
deliberately beat their heads against trees, rocks,
posts, or brush. . . . In extreme cases of intense
infestation a sheep may even kill itself in a frenzied
endeavor to gain respite from the aggravation."[4]

When a swarm of nose flies appears, sheep panic. They run. They hide. They toss their heads up and down for hours. They forget to eat. They aren't able to sleep. Ewes stop milking, and lambs stop growing. The entire flock can be disrupted, even destroyed by the presence of a few flies.

For this reason, the shepherd anoints the sheep. He covers their heads with an oil-like repellent. The fragrance keeps the insects at bay and the flock at peace.

At peace, that is, until mating season. Most of the year, sheep are calm, passive animals. But during mating season, everything changes. The rams put the "ram" in *rambunctious*. They strut around the pasture and flex their necks, trying to win the attention of the new gal on the block. When a ram catches her eye, he tosses his head back and says, "I want ewe, baby." About that time her boyfriend shows up and tells her to go someplace safe. "Ewe better move, sweetie. This could get ugly." The two rams lower their heads and POW! An old-fashioned head butt breaks out.

To prevent injury, the shepherd anoints the rams. He smears a slippery, greasy substance over the nose and head. This lubricant causes them to glance off rather than crash into each other.

They still tend to get hurt, however. And these wounds are the third reason the shepherd anoints the sheep.

Most of the wounds the shepherd treats are simply the result of living in a pasture. Thorns prick or rocks cut or a sheep rubs its head too hard against a tree. Sheep get hurt. As a result, the shepherd regularly, often daily, inspects the sheep, searching for cuts and abrasions. He doesn't want the cut to worsen. He doesn't want today's wound to become tomorrow's infection.

Neither does God. Just like sheep, we have

wounds, but ours are wounds of the heart that come from disappointment after disappointment. If we're not careful, these wounds lead to bitterness. And so just like sheep, we need to be treated. "He made us, and we belong to him; we are his people, the sheep he tends" (Ps. 100:3).

Sheep aren't the only ones who need preventive care, and sheep aren't the only ones who need a healing touch. We also get irritated with each other, butt heads, and then get wounded. Many of our disappointments in life begin as irritations. The large portion of our problems are not lion-sized attacks, but rather the day-to-day swarm of frustrations and mishaps and heartaches. You don't get invited to the dinner party. You don't make the team. You don't get the scholarship. Your boss doesn't notice your hard work. Your husband doesn't notice your new dress. Your neighbor doesn't notice the mess in his yard. You find yourself more irritable, more gloomy, more . . . well, more hurt.

Like the sheep, you don't sleep well, you don't eat well. You may even hit your head against a tree a few times.

Or you may hit your head against a person. It's amazing how hardheaded we can be with each other. Some of our deepest hurts come from butting heads with people.

Like the sheep, the rest of our wounds come just from living in the pasture. The pasture of the sheep, however, is much more appealing. The sheep have to face wounds from thorns and this-tles. We have to face aging, loss, and illness. Some of us face betrayal and injustice. Live long enough in this world, and most of us will face deep, deep hurts of some kind or another.

So we, like the sheep, get wounded. And we, like the sheep, have a shepherd. Remember the words we read? "We belong to him; we are his people, the sheep he tends" (Ps. 100:3). He will do for you what the shepherd does for the sheep. He will tend to you.

If you will let him. How? How do you let him? The steps are so simple.

First, go to him. David would trust his wounds to no other person but God. He said, "You anoint my head with oil." Not, "your prophets," "your teachers," or "your counselors." Others may guide us to God. Others may help us understand God. But no one does the work of God, for only God can heal. God "heals the brokenhearted" (Ps. 147:3).

Have you taken your disappointments to God? You've shared them with your neighbor, your relatives, your friends. But have you taken them to God? James says, "Anyone who is having troubles should pray" (James 5:13).

Before you go anywhere else with your disappointments, go to God.

Maybe you don't want to trouble God with your hurts. *After all, he's got famines and pestilence and wars; he won't care about my little struggles,* you think. Why don't you let him decide that? He cared enough about a wedding to provide the wine. He cared enough about Peter's tax payment to give him a coin. He cared enough about the woman at the well to give her answers. "He cares about you" (1 Pet. 5:7).

Your first step is to go to the right person. Go to God. Your second step is to assume the right posture. Bow before God.

In order to be anointed, the sheep must stand still, lower their heads, and let the shepherd do his work. Peter urges us to "be humble under God's powerful hand so he will lift you up when the right time comes" (1 Pet. 5:6).

When we come to God, we make requests; we don't make demands. We come with high hopes and a humble heart. We state what we want, but we pray for what is right. And if God gives us the prison of Rome instead of the mission of Spain, we accept it because we know "God will always give what is right to his people who cry to him night and day, and he will not be slow to answer them" (Luke 18:7).

We go to him. We bow before him, and we *trust in him.*

The sheep doesn't understand why the oil repels the flies. The sheep doesn't understand how the oil heals the wounds. In fact, all the sheep knows is that something happens in the presence of the shepherd. And that's all we need to know as well. "Lord, I give myself to you; my God, I trust you" (Ps. 25:1–2).

Go.

Bow.

Trust.

Worth a try, don't you think?

# MY CUP RUNS OVER

*Our cup
overflows with blessings.*

Is an overflowing cup full? Absolutely. The wine reaches the rim and then tumbles over the edge. The goblet is not large enough to contain the quantity. According to David, our hearts are not large enough to contain the blessings that God wants to give. He pours and pours until they literally flow over the edge and down on the table.

The overflowing cup was a powerful symbol in the days of David. Hosts in the ancient East used it to send a message to the guest. As long as the cup was kept full, the guest knew he was welcome. But when the cup sat empty, the host was hinting that the hour was late. On those occasions, however, when the host really enjoyed the company of the person, he filled the cup to overflowing. He didn't stop when the wine reached the rim; he kept pouring until the liquid ran over the edge of the cup and down on the table.[5]

TRAVELING LIGHT

Have you ever wondered why God gives so much? We could exist on far less. He could have left the world flat and gray; we wouldn't have known the difference. But he didn't.

> *He splashed orange in the sunrise*
> *and cast the sky in blue.*
> *And if you love to see geese as they gather,*
> *chances are you'll see that too.*
> *Did he have to make the squirrel's tail furry?*
> *Was he obliged to make the birds sing?*
> *And the funny way that chickens scurry*
> *or the majesty of thunder when it rings?*

*Why give a flower fragrance? Why give food its taste?*

*Could it be*

*he loves to see*

*That look upon your face?*

If we give gifts to show our love, how much more would he? If we—speckled with foibles and greed—love to give gifts, how much more does God, pure and perfect God, enjoy giving gifts to us?

He Chose the Nails

So the next time a sunrise steals your breath or a meadow of flowers leaves you speechless, remain that way. Say nothing and listen as heaven whispers, "Do you like it? I did it just for you."

I'm about to tell you something you may find hard to believe. . . . Here it is: If you were the only person on earth, the earth would look exactly the same. The Himalayas would still have their drama and the Caribbean would still have its charm. The sun would still nestle behind the Rockies in the evenings and spray light on the desert in the mornings. If you were the sole pilgrim on this globe, God would not diminish its beauty one degree.

Because he did it all for you . . . and he's waiting for you to discover his gift. . . . He's waiting for your eyes to pop and your heart to stop. He's waiting for the moment between the dropping of the jaw and the leap of the heart. For in that silence he leans forward and whispers: I did it just for you.

Find such love hard to believe? That's okay. . . . Just because we can't imagine God's giving us sunsets, don't think God doesn't do it. God's thoughts are higher than ours. God's ways are greater than ours. And sometimes, out of his great wisdom, our Father in heaven gives us a piece of heaven just to show he cares.

THE GREAT HOUSE OF GOD

# SURELY GOODNESS
# AND MERCY SHALL FOLLOW ME
# ALL THE DAYS OF MY LIFE

*Goodness to supply every want.*

*Mercy to forgive every sin.*

*Goodness to provide.*

*Mercy to pardon.*

———

—F. B. MEYER

*S*urely goodness and mercy shall follow me all the days of my life."

This must be one of the sweetest phrases ever penned. Can we read it from a few other translations?

"Goodness and love unfailing, these will follow me all the days of my life, and I shall dwell in the house of the LORD my whole life long" (NEB).

"I know that your goodness and love will be with me all my life; and your house will be my home as long as I live" (TEV).

"Your beauty and love chase after me every day of my life. I'm back home in the house of Yahweh for the rest of my life" (MSG).

To read the verse is to open a box of jewels. Each word sparkles and begs to be examined in the face of our doubts: *goodness, mercy, all the days, dwell in the house of the* LORD, *forever.* They sweep in on insecurities like a SWAT team on a terrorist.

Look at the first word: *surely.* David didn't say, "*Maybe* goodness and mercy shall follow me." Or "*Possibly* goodness and mercy shall follow me." Or "*I have a hunch* that goodness and mercy shall follow me." David could have used one of those phrases. But he didn't. He believed in a sure God, who makes sure promises and provides a sure foundation.

Our moods may shift, but God's doesn't. Our minds may change, but God's doesn't. Our devotion may falter, but God's never does. Even if we are faithless, he is faithful, for he cannot betray himself (2 Tim. 2:13). He is a sure God. And because he is a sure God, we can state confidently, "Surely goodness and mercy shall follow me all the days of my life."

And what follows the word *surely?* "Goodness and mercy." If the Lord is the shepherd who leads the flock, goodness and mercy are the two sheep-dogs that guard the rear of the flock. Goodness *and* mercy. Not goodness alone, for we are sinners in need of mercy. Not mercy alone, for we are fragile, in need of goodness. We need them both.

Goodness and mercy—the celestial escort of God's flock. If that duo doesn't reinforce your faith, try this phrase: "all the days of my life."

What a huge statement. Look at the size of it! Goodness and mercy follow the child of God each and every day! Think of the days that lie ahead. What do you see? Days at home with only toddlers? God will be at your side. Days in a dead-end job? He will walk you through. Days of loneliness? He will take your hand. Surely goodness and mercy shall follow me—not some, not most, not nearly all—but all the days of my life.

And what will he do during those days? (Here is my favorite word.) He will "follow" you.

What a surprising way to describe God! We're accustomed to a God who remains in one place. A God who sits enthroned in the heavens and rules and ordains. David, however, envisions a mobile and active God. Dare we do the same? Dare we envision a God who follows us? Who pursues us? Who chases us? Who tracks us down and wins us over? Who follows us with "goodness and mercy" all the days of our lives? . . .

God is the God who follows. I wonder . . . have you sensed him following you? We often miss him. We don't know our Helper when he is near. But he comes.

Through the kindness of a stranger. The majesty of a sunset. The mystery of romance. Through the question of a child or the commitment of a spouse. Through a word well spoken or a touch well timed, have you sensed his presence?

If so, then release your doubts. Set them down. Be encumbered by them no longer. You are no candidate for insecurity. You are no longer a client of timidity. You can trust God. He has given his love to you; why don't you give your doubts to him? . . .

God gives us himself. Even when we choose our hovel over his house and our trash over his grace, still he follows. Never forcing us. Never leaving us. Patiently persistent. Faithfully present. Using all of his power to convince us that he is who he is and that he can be trusted to lead us home.

His goodness and mercy will follow us all the days of our lives.

TRAVELING LIGHT

# I WILL DWELL
## IN THE HOUSE OF THE
## LORD FOREVER

*This isn't just any house.*

*It is our Father's house.*

W here will you live forever? In the house of the Lord. If his house is your "forever house," what does that make this earthly house? You got it! Short-term housing. This is not our home. "Our homeland is in heaven" (Phil. 3:20).

This explains the homesickness we feel.

Have you ever longed to be home? May I share a time when I did? I was spending the summer of my nineteenth year working in northern Georgia. The folks in that region are very nice, but no one is too nice to a door-to-door salesman. There were times that summer when I was so lonely for home I felt my bones would melt.

One of those occasions came on the side of a country road. The hour was late, and I was lost. I'd stopped to pull out a flashlight and a map. To my right was a farmhouse. In the farmhouse was a family. I knew it was a family because I could see them. Right through the big plate-glass window, I could see the mother and father and boy and girl. Norman Rockwell would have placed them on a canvas. The mom was spooning out food, and the dad was telling a story, and the kids were laughing, and it was all I could do to keep from ringing the doorbell and asking for a place at the table. I felt so far from home.

What I felt that night, some of you have felt ever since . . .

your husband died.

your child was buried.

you learned about the lump in your breast or the spot in your lung.

Some of you have felt far from home ever since your home fell apart.

The twists and turns of life have a way of reminding us—we aren't home here. This is not our homeland. We aren't fluent in the languages of disease and death. The culture confuses the heart, the noise disrupts our sleep, and we feel far from home.

And, you know what? That's OK.

You have an eternal address fixed in your mind. God has "set eternity in the hearts of men" (Eccles. 3:11 NIV). Down deep you know you are not home yet.

So be careful not to act like you are.

Traveling Light

Though our eyes are fixed on heaven, for some of us the journey has been long. Very long and stormy. In no way do I wish to minimize the difficulties that you have had to face along the way. Some of you have shouldered burdens that few of us could

ever carry. You have bid farewell to life-long partners.
You have been robbed of life-long dreams. You
have been given bodies that can't sustain your
spirit. You have spouses who can't tolerate your
faith. You have bills that outnumber the paychecks
and challenges that outweigh the strength.

And you are tired.

It's hard for you to see the City in the midst of
the storms. The desire to pull over to the side of
the road and get out entices you. You want to go
on, but some days the road seems so long.

Remember this: God never said that the journey would be easy, but he did say that the arrival
would be worthwhile. He may not do what you
want, but he will do what is right . . . and best. He's
the Father of forward motion. Trust him. He will
get you home. And the trials of the trip will be lost
in the joys of the feast.

IN THE EYE OF THE STORM

# CLOSING THOUGHTS

*The world rams at your door;*

*Jesus taps at your door.*

The mark of a sheep is its ability to hear the Shepherd's voice.

"The sheep listen to his voice. He calls his own sheep by name and leads them out."

The mark of a disciple is his or her ability to hear the Master's voice.

"Here I am! I stand at the door and knock. If anyone hears my voice and opens the door, I will come in and eat with him, and he with me."

The world rams at your door; Jesus taps at your door. The voices scream for your allegiance; Jesus softly and tenderly requests it. The world promises flashy pleasure; Jesus promises a quiet dinner . . . with God. "I will come in and eat."

Which voice do you hear?

Let me state something important. There is never a time during which Jesus is not speaking. Never. There is never a place in which Jesus is not present. Never. There is never a room so dark . . . a lounge so sensual . . . an office so sophisticated . . . that the ever-present, ever-pursuing, relentlessly tender Friend is not there, tapping gently on the doors of our hearts—waiting to be invited in.

Few hear his voice. Fewer still open the door.

But never interpret our numbness as his absence. For amidst the fleeting promises of pleasure is the timeless promise of his presence.

"Surely I am with you always, to the very end of the age."

"Never will I leave you; never will I forsake you."

There is no chorus so loud that the voice of God cannot be heard . . . if we will but listen. . . .

A day is coming when everyone will hear his voice. A day is coming when all the other voices will be silenced; his voice—and his voice only—will be heard.

Some will hear his voice for the very first time. It's not that he never spoke, it's just that they never listened. For these, God's voice will be the voice of a stranger. They will hear it once—and never hear it again. They will spend eternity fending off the voices they followed on earth.

But others will be called from their graves by a familiar voice. For they are sheep who know their shepherd. They are servants who opened the door when Jesus knocked.

Now the door will open again. Only this time, it won't be Jesus who walks into our house; it will be we, who walk into his.

IN THE EYE OF THE STORM

# ENDNOTES

1 Donald W. McCullough, *The Trivialization of God: The Dangerous Illusion of a Manageable Deity* (Colorado Springs: NavPress, 1995), 66.

2 From "Worrier and Warrior," a sermon by Ted Schroder, Christ Episcopal Church, San Antonio, Texas, on 10 April 1994.

3 Charles W. Slemming, *He Leadeth Me: The Shepherd's Life in Palestine* (Fort Washington, PA.: Christian Literature Crusade, 1964), quoted in Charles R. Swindoll, *Living Beyond the Daily Grind, Book 1: Reflections on the Songs and Sayings in Scripture* (Dallas: Word Publishing, 1988), 77–78.

4 Phillip Keller, *A Shepherd Looks at Psalm 23* (Grand Rapids, Mich.: Zondervan Publishing, 1970; reprint, in *Phillip Keller: The Inspirational Writings*, New York: Inspirational Press, 1993), 99 (page citation is to the reprint edition).

5 From a sermon entitled "God's Antidote to Your Hurt" by Rick Warren.

# ACKNOWLEDGMENTS

Grateful acknowledgment is made to the following publishers for permission to reprint this copyrighted material. All copyrights are held by the author, Max Lucado.

*The Applause of Heaven* (Nashville: Word, 1990).

*In the Eye of the Storm* (Nashville: Word, 1991).

*He Still Moves Stones* (Nashville: Word, 1993).

*When God Whispers Your Name* (Nashville: Word, 1994).

*A Gentle Thunder* (Nashville: Word, 1995).

*In the Grip of Grace* (Nashville: Word, 1996).

*The Great House of God* (Nashville: Word, 1997).

*He Chose the Nails* (Nashville: Word, 2000).

*Traveling Light* (Nashville: W Publishing Group, 2001).

"He Reminded Us of You" (a prayer for a friend).